1

THE LANGUAGE OF WOMEN

THE LANGUAGE OF WOMEN

Understand What She Really Means

DARRIN ELFORD

DARRIN ELFORD
PREMIUM BOOKS

Acknowledgements

Writing this book has been an incredible journey, and I am deeply grateful to everyone who has contributed to its creation.

First and foremost, I want to thank the women in my life—my family, friends, and colleagues—who have generously shared their insights, experiences, and wisdom about communication and emotional expression. Without your honest conversations and your willingness to open up about the complexities of female communication, this book would not have been possible. You have taught me more than I could ever express in words.

I also want to express my gratitude to my loved ones, whose patience, understanding, and constant support have been invaluable throughout this process. Your empathy and ability to listen with an open heart have been my inspiration for exploring the language of women in such depth.

A special thank you goes to my readers—those who have shared their feedback, stories, and challenges about understanding the language of women. Your willingness to engage with this material has been motivating and has helped me refine the content to better serve those seeking to build stronger, more empathetic relationships.

Lastly, to anyone who has ever struggled to understand the unspoken messages behind words, I hope this book helps illuminate the complexities of communication, allowing you to connect more deeply and meaningfully with the women in your life. This book is for you.

Thank you all for your support, encouragement, and belief in this project.

Table of Contents

Introduction

If you're holding this book, it's because you're ready to better understand the women in your life and communicate with them on a deeper level. Whether you're a partner, friend, father, or colleague, unlocking the language of women can transform your relationships and help you build stronger, more meaningful connections.

As an expert in communication, I've spent years studying how men and women express themselves. It's clear that the way women communicate often doesn't follow the simple, direct approach many men are used to. Women tend to communicate with more nuance, using not just words but also body language, tone, and emotional cues to express their feelings and needs.

In this book, I'll guide you through the process of understanding what women really mean when they speak—beyond the words. We'll explore the **differences in communication styles** between men and women, dive into the hidden meanings behind common phrases, and teach you how to interpret **non-verbal signals** like body language and emotional cues.

By the end of this book, you'll be able to decode what she's really saying, even when she's not saying it directly. You'll learn how to listen with both your ears and your eyes, how to read between the lines, and how to connect with her on a level that's built on mutual understanding and trust.

This isn't just about learning a few tricks to "figure her out." It's about mastering a communication style that will help you foster deeper relationships with women in all aspects of your life. So, if you're ready to improve your communication and truly understand the women around you, let's get started.

1

Male and Female Communication Foundations

The Science of Communication

To understand the differences in communication between men and women, we need to first look at the science behind how we communicate. Our brains and bodies are wired differently, and these differences impact how we express ourselves, listen, and interpret the world around us. Let's dive into the biological and psychological factors that shape communication.

Biological and Psychological Differences in Communication

At a basic level, men and women's brains function differently, which influences how they communicate. Men's brains tend to be more specialized, while women's brains are more integrated. For example, women often use both hemispheres of the brain when speaking, while men may rely more on just one hemisphere. This means women are naturally better at multitasking in communication, using both verbal and non-verbal cues simultaneously.

The difference is also tied to the way emotions are processed. Women generally have more activity in the emotional centers of the brain, particularly the areas responsible for empathy and emotional expression. This means that women are more likely to connect their emotions to their words. When a woman communicates, she may be expressing not just the facts, but also how she feels about the situation.

Men, on the other hand, have a brain structure that favors logical and linear thinking. They tend to approach problems and communication with a focus on facts and solutions, which is why they often come across as more direct and to the point. This isn't because men don't care about emotions, but because their brain functions often prioritize resolving issues over expressing emotional states.

How Hormones Impact Language and Tone

Hormones also play a significant role in how men and women communicate. Testosterone, the primary male hormone, promotes assertiveness and focus, which is why men tend to speak more directly and with a goal-oriented mindset. When men are conversing, especially in problem-solving situations, their language tends to be more straightforward, as they're often thinking about how to fix the problem at hand.

On the other hand, women have higher levels of estrogen, which promotes nurturing behaviors and emotional connection. This can explain why women's language is often more emotionally expressive and nuanced. Estrogen encourages women to communicate in ways that foster connection, support, and empathy, making them more likely to use language that reflects their feelings and relationships.

The interplay of these hormones can also affect tone. A woman's tone of voice may fluctuate with her emotions, signalling whether she's happy, upset, or excited. For men, the tone may remain more consistent, as they are often more focused on the message than the emotional state behind it. This can sometimes lead to misunderstandings, as women may feel that the tone of a conversation is as important as the words being spoken, while men may not immediately pick up on those emotional shifts.

How These Differences Shape Conversational Dynamics

These biological and hormonal differences shape how men and women engage in conversation. Because women are often more in touch with their emotions and use more expressive language, their conversations may be longer and more relational. They are more likely to talk about feelings, experiences, and emotions, often looking for validation and understanding from others.

Men, on the other hand, are more likely to focus on solving problems or getting to the point. When a man is asked a question, he may jump straight into providing a solution rather than listening to the emotional context behind the question. Women, however, may see this as dismissive or disconnected, as they are more focused on the emotional aspect of the conversation.

This dynamic can sometimes create frustration in communication. Women may feel that men don't "get" them emotionally, while men may feel that women are overcomplicating things or asking for help when none is needed. Recognizing that these differences are rooted in biology and brain function can help both sides understand that neither approach is wrong—it's just different.

Why Women Tend to Use More Emotional Language

The emotional wiring of women's brains leads them to use more emotionally driven language. When a woman speaks, she may include more descriptive words about how she feels and what she's experiencing. This is not just a matter of being "emotional" or "dramatic"; it's how her brain processes information. Women often think about relationships and emotional connections when communicating, and their language reflects this.

For example, a woman might say, "I'm really upset about how things went down yesterday," not just to express a fact, but to communicate the emotional impact it had on her. She's seeking understanding and empathy. This kind of language helps her feel connected to others and reinforces the relationships she values.

For men, emotional language might feel less natural or unnecessary. They're more inclined to speak about events and facts directly, focusing on what happened rather than how it made them feel. This difference can lead to misunderstandings if both parties don't recognize where the other is coming from. While a woman might feel that emotional expression is important for building intimacy, a man may see it as irrelevant to the issue at hand.

The Male Tendency to Focus on Problem-Solving Language

Men, as a result of their brain structure and hormonal influences, often approach communication with a solution-oriented mindset. When a problem arises, men are more likely to focus on finding a solution rather than discussing the emotions surrounding it. This is why, when a woman shares a problem with a man, he might immediately suggest a way to fix it, even if she's not asking for a solution. She may just want to talk about her feelings, not hear how to fix the situation.

For example, if a woman says, "I'm feeling overwhelmed at work," a man might quickly respond with, "You should delegate tasks or talk to your boss about your workload." While this is a logical, solution-driven response, it might not meet her emotional need for support and understanding. She may be looking for empathy and someone to simply listen to her feelings, rather than being told what to do.

The key here is understanding that both approaches are valid, but they serve different purposes. Women often communicate to express their feelings and connect emotionally, while men communicate to solve problems and provide solutions. Recognizing these differences allows both parties to adjust their expectations and approach to communication.

In this section we've laid the groundwork for understanding why men and women communicate the way they do. By recognizing the biological, hormonal, and psychological factors at play, you can begin to appreciate the nuances in how women express themselves and learn to communicate in a way that bridges the gap between these two styles. The next step is learning to decode what's being said and, perhaps more importantly, what's being left unsaid.

Recognizing Non-Verbal Cues

Communication isn't just about the words we speak. In fact, much of what we convey comes through non-verbal cues—body language, facial expressions, tone, and even silence. Women, in particular, often rely heavily on these non-verbal signals to communicate emotions, needs, and intentions. Understanding these subtle cues can provide you with a much deeper insight into what she really means. Let's explore how to recognize and interpret these non-verbal signals effectively.

The Importance of Body Language and Facial Expressions

Body language and facial expressions are two of the most powerful tools in communication. In many cases, they can reveal more about a person's true feelings than words ever could. In fact, studies have shown that around 60-70% of communication is non-verbal. This means that what you see—how someone moves, stands, and expresses themselves physically—speaks volumes about how they're feeling.

Women often communicate their emotions through their body language. For example, crossed arms might indicate defensiveness or discomfort, while leaning forward could signal interest or engagement. A smile, however small, often communicates warmth and openness. When you pay attention to these physical signs, you can better understand the emotions and intentions behind what is being said.

Facial expressions, in particular, are essential in reading non-verbal cues. A lot can be understood from just a simple glance. While words can be carefully chosen and controlled, our faces often give away what we're really feeling, sometimes without us even realizing it. A slight furrow of the brow or a small sigh can tell you much more than a sentence ever could.

Subtle Facial Expressions that Convey Unspoken Messages

A person's face is one of the most expressive parts of the body, and subtle facial expressions often carry deep emotional meaning. Even small changes in a woman's facial expression can indicate a range of feelings, from happiness and excitement to confusion or frustration. Here are a few examples of what to look for:

- **Raised eyebrows:** Often a sign of surprise, curiosity, or interest. If a woman raises her eyebrows while listening to you, she's likely engaged and interested in the conversation.
- **Tightened lips:** This can indicate discomfort or disagreement. If her lips are pressed together in a thin line, it's possible that she's holding back her true feelings, perhaps because she doesn't feel safe to express them fully.
- **Eye contact (or lack of):** Eye contact is a powerful tool in communication. Direct eye contact can show trust, attentiveness, and connection. However,

avoiding eye contact may signal discomfort, avoidance, or even a desire to end the conversation.

These facial expressions, even if they seem subtle, are crucial for understanding the emotional tone of the conversation. Pay attention to these cues, and you'll start to notice patterns that give you a clearer idea of what's going on beneath the surface.

How Posture and Gestures Add Depth to What's Being Said

Posture and gestures are also integral parts of non-verbal communication. A woman's body language can amplify the meaning of her words—or even contradict them. For example, if she's speaking about something exciting but her posture is slumped or closed off, this might indicate that she's not as engaged or excited as her words suggest.

Here are some important things to look for in her posture and gestures:

- **Open vs. closed posture:** An open posture—standing or sitting with uncrossed arms, facing you directly—indicates openness and willingness to communicate. A closed posture, such as crossed arms or avoiding eye contact, can signal defensiveness, discomfort, or disengagement.
- **Leaning in or away:** If she leans in toward you while talking, it's usually a sign of interest and emotional involvement. Leaning back or away may suggest that she's emotionally distancing herself or that she's not fully engaged in the conversation.
- **Gestures:** Hand movements, nods, and even the way she holds her hands can provide a deeper layer of meaning. For example, if she's talking about something she's passionate about and uses a lot of hand gestures, it indicates that the subject matter is important to her. If her hands are clenched or fidgeting, she might be feeling nervous, anxious, or frustrated.

Paying attention to her posture and gestures will give you additional context to the words she's saying. These physical cues add depth to the conversation, allowing you to understand her emotional state more clearly.

Understanding Tone and Pitch

The way something is said can be just as important as what is being said. Tone and pitch—the qualities of sound in the voice—play a huge role in interpreting meaning. A woman might use the same words, but her tone can completely change the message she's sending. This is particularly important in understanding emotions, as tone and pitch can convey a wide range of feelings, from happiness to irritation, sadness, or even sarcasm.

- **Tone:** Tone refers to the emotional quality of the voice. A soft, warm tone typically signals affection, calmness, or understanding. A sharp, curt tone may suggest frustration, impatience, or even anger. When a woman's tone shifts, it's an indicator of her emotional state. If her tone is rising in pitch, it might indicate excitement or frustration, while a lowered tone could suggest sadness or tiredness.

- **Pitch:** Pitch refers to how high or low the voice sounds. A higher pitch often suggests excitement, nervousness, or anxiety, while a lower pitch may indicate calmness, seriousness, or authority. Sudden shifts in pitch can signal emotional changes as well. For instance, if her voice suddenly becomes higher in pitch when discussing something sensitive, it could signal a mix of excitement and vulnerability.

Understanding the role of tone and pitch can help you interpret the deeper meaning behind her words. For instance, if she says, "That's fine," but her tone is sharp and her pitch is high, you might want to read between the lines. She's probably not as okay with the situation as the words suggest.

Conclusion

Non-verbal cues are an essential part of communication and recognizing them will help you understand a woman's true feelings, even when she's not saying everything out loud. By paying attention to her body language, facial expressions, posture, and tone, you can gain a clearer picture of what's really going on beneath the surface. As you develop your ability to interpret these signals, you'll find yourself connecting with her on a much deeper level - one that goes far beyond just words.

Common Misunderstandings in Communication

In any relationship, whether it's romantic, professional, or social, misunderstandings are bound to happen. The way men and women communicate can sometimes lead to confusion, frustration, and even conflict. Many of these misunderstandings arise from the natural differences in how we interpret words, tone, body language, and context. Understanding these common pitfalls can help you avoid them and create more effective, empathetic communication. Let's dive into some of the key misunderstandings that often occur between men and women.

Assumptions vs. Interpretations

One of the most common sources of miscommunication is the difference between **assumptions** and **interpretations**. An assumption happens when someone jumps to a conclusion without fully understanding the other person's intent or emotional state. An interpretation, on the other hand, is how you read a message, based on the available information and context.

Men often make the mistake of assuming that when a woman says something, it's simply about the facts—no more, no less. For instance, if she says, "I'm really tired," he might assume she's just stating a fact and doesn't need anything further. He may not realize that she's actually expressing a deeper need for support, comfort, or empathy.

Women, on the other hand, may interpret a man's words or actions differently based on his tone or body language. If a man is quiet or seems distracted, a woman might assume he's upset with her or doesn't care. This is often an **interpretation** of the situation based on her emotional state, rather than a true reflection of what's happening.

The key to overcoming these misunderstandings is to recognize the difference between assumptions (which are often based on incomplete information) and interpretations (which involve interpreting a situation through personal emotional lenses). By being mindful of this distinction, you can avoid jumping to conclusions and improve your understanding of each other's intentions.

Why Men Often Misinterpret Women's Tone and Gestures

One of the main reasons men tend to misinterpret women's communication is because they often don't pick up on the emotional nuances in a woman's tone or body language. As mentioned earlier, men generally focus more on the content of a conversation, while women are often more attuned to the emotional undertones.

For example, a woman might say, "That's fine," but if her tone is sharp and her posture is closed off, men may misinterpret this as her truly being fine, even though she may be upset. Men often rely on words alone to determine the meaning of a statement, and they might overlook the body language or tone that signals a deeper emotional state. Because women tend to express emotions more openly through tone and gestures, it's essential for men to learn how to read these cues to better understand what is really being communicated.

In these situations, men may feel confused, thinking that the words should be enough, but they're missing the emotional context. The key here is to recognize that women often communicate on multiple levels, using not just words but tone, gestures, and body language to express how they feel.

How Women May Expect a Deeper Level of Understanding

Women often expect a deeper level of understanding from their partners, friends, and colleagues. They don't just want their words to be heard; they want to feel understood emotionally. When women communicate, they may be looking for empathy, connection, and emotional support rather than just problem-solving or simple answers.

For instance, if a woman talks about feeling overwhelmed at work, she may not be seeking a solution right away. What she may truly want is for her partner to listen and acknowledge her feelings. She might expect him to pick up on the emotional weight behind her words and respond with empathy rather than jumping straight into fixing the problem.

This expectation can lead to misunderstandings because men, who are often focused on solutions, may not immediately recognize the need for emotional understanding. To avoid this, it's important to realize that women's communication is often about expressing their emotions and seeking validation, not just sharing information.

Why Context Matters

Context is another key factor in effective communication. The meaning of what someone says can change dramatically depending on the situation, environment, or emotional state of the person speaking. A statement made in one context may have an entirely different meaning in another.

For example, if a woman says, "I'm fine" after a stressful day at work, the context of her emotional state—tired, frustrated, or overwhelmed—can give you a better understanding of what she's truly feeling. Without considering the context, it's easy to misinterpret her words as simply a neutral statement.

Likewise, if a man is quiet during a conversation, he might be deep in thought or just processing information, but if his partner doesn't understand the context—such as his emotional state or the situation he's in—she might incorrectly assume he's upset or uninterested.

Context is crucial in understanding the full meaning behind a statement. Always ask yourself: what else is going on in the moment that might explain why she's saying what she's saying? Is she stressed, tired, or feeling vulnerable? By considering the context of a conversation, you can gain a deeper understanding of the message being communicated.

The Impact of Setting and Emotional States

The setting and emotional state of both parties can greatly influence how communication unfolds. If either person is feeling anxious, stressed, or upset, the message may come across more negatively than intended. The setting also plays a role—whether you're at home, in a busy restaurant, or in a quiet office, the environment can impact how open and relaxed both people feel during the conversation.

For example, if a woman is upset about something and is trying to talk about it in a loud, chaotic environment, her message may get lost in the noise. Similarly, if she's having a difficult conversation with a man while he's preoccupied or distracted, he may not be fully present to understand the emotional depth of her words.

It's important to recognize when either person is in a heightened emotional state and be aware of how that can affect communication. A calm, private setting can foster better understanding, while a stressful environment may require extra patience and attention to tone, body language, and emotional context.

Learning to Ask Questions for Clarity

One of the most effective ways to prevent misunderstandings is to ask questions for clarity. Instead of assuming you know what someone means, take the time to check in with them and ensure you're both on the same page.

For instance, if you're unsure whether a woman is upset, instead of assuming based on her tone or body language, you can ask, "I noticed you seem a little tense—are you okay?" or "It sounds like something is bothering you. Do you want to talk about it?" These questions open up space for deeper communication and prevent the common pitfalls of assumption and misinterpretation.

It's also important to practice active listening. Instead of jumping to conclusions or offering solutions right away, take a moment to really listen to her words, tone, and body language. Asking clarifying questions shows that you care about understanding her fully and are committed to improving the way you communicate together.

Conclusion

In this chapter, we've explored some of the most common misunderstandings that arise in male and female communication. By being aware of the differences in how we interpret tone, gestures, context, and emotional states, we can avoid many of these pitfalls and improve our relationships. By asking questions for clarity and recognizing when assumptions are being made, you can create a more empathetic, understanding, and effective communication style that benefits both parties. The next step is learning how to create deeper connections and enhance your understanding of each other's needs.

2

Decoding What She's Really Saying

The Power of indirect Communication

One of the most notable differences between male and female communication is the tendency for women to communicate indirectly. While men often prefer straightforwardness, women often rely on subtlety, hints, and implied meanings to convey their thoughts, emotions, and desires. This indirect communication style can sometimes be confusing for men, especially when they're used to receiving clear and direct messages. Understanding the reasons behind this tendency and learning how to interpret it is a key step in fully understanding the language of women.

Women's Tendency to Speak Indirectly

Women often express themselves in a more indirect way compared to men. This can be seen in how they phrase requests, concerns, or even compliments. Instead of saying something directly, like "I'm upset," a woman might say, "I don't know… it's just been a long day." Or rather than directly asking for help, she might say, "I could really use a hand right now," without specifically requesting support.

This indirect communication doesn't mean that women are being secretive or unclear on purpose. Rather, it reflects a tendency to be more nuanced in how they express themselves. This style allows them to communicate complex emotions without confronting others directly, which can feel uncomfortable or aggressive.

Understanding why women use this indirect approach can help you read between the lines. In many cases, this method of communication is a way to protect themselves from confrontation or to avoid coming across as too demanding.

Why Women Often Communicate Indirectly to Avoid Conflict

One of the primary reasons women communicate indirectly is to avoid conflict. Many women are socialized to be more emotionally attuned to the feelings of others, which can make them more reluctant to express their dissatisfaction or needs in a way that might cause tension or upset someone. Direct confrontation can feel aggressive, and women may worry that being too blunt will damage the relationship or create unnecessary conflict.

For example, if a woman is frustrated with something her partner has done, she might not directly say, "You never listen to me." Instead, she may say, "I've noticed that lately I feel like I'm always the one doing all the talking." This indirect approach is often a way to open the door to a conversation without immediately escalating it into an argument.

By communicating indirectly, women often hope to give their partner the opportunity to pick up on the dissatisfaction and address it without making a scene or causing tension. This style of communication is designed to keep things peaceful, even though it may not always lead to the most straightforward resolution.

Understanding the Need for Subtlety in Expressing Dissatisfaction

For women, subtlety can be an important tool in expressing dissatisfaction. Being too blunt or forward about negative feelings can sometimes feel uncomfortable or overly confrontational. Instead of voicing frustration directly, women might drop hints or use language that isn't as forceful but still conveys their concerns. This allows them to express their feelings without feeling vulnerable or overly exposed.

A woman might say, "It's fine, I'll just handle it myself," when she's actually feeling overwhelmed or unsupported. In these cases, she's hinting at her dissatisfaction, but the phrasing is indirect enough to avoid direct confrontation.

This subtlety is a way of testing how much the other person is paying attention. It's also a way of softening the impact of her dissatisfaction.

If you learn to pick up on these subtle cues, you can respond in a way that acknowledges her feelings without making her feel defensive or cornered. For instance, instead of brushing off her statement, you could ask, "It sounds like you're feeling a bit stressed. Is there something I can do to help?"

How to Interpret Hints and Implied Meanings

The key to understanding indirect communication is learning to recognize the **hints** and **implied meanings** behind what is said. Women often won't say exactly what they mean outright, but they'll use language, tone, and body language to suggest what's really going on. By paying attention to these subtle cues, you can begin to interpret what she might be feeling or trying to communicate.

For instance, if she says, "It's really quiet in here today," it may not be a simple observation. She might actually be hinting that she's feeling lonely or disconnected. If she says, "I could really use some help around here," she's probably implying that she's feeling overwhelmed and wants assistance, but she's not asking directly.

Recognizing these hints requires you to listen carefully—not just to the words, but also to the tone, body language, and context. Understanding what's not being said can give you much more insight into her feelings and needs than you might realize.

Identifying What's Left Unsaid But Implied

Another key aspect of indirect communication is understanding what's **left unsaid but implied**. Women often don't feel the need to say everything directly. Instead, they might expect their partner to read between the lines and pick up on what's not explicitly stated. This can be tricky because it requires an understanding of the emotional context and the relationship dynamic.

For example, if she says, "I haven't heard from you in a while," she might not just be making an observation about your communication habits. What she may actually be implying is that she feels neglected or that she values your attention more than you've been giving her. By recognizing that this isn't just a comment about the passage of time, you can respond in a way that addresses her deeper emotional need—by reassuring her that you care and will make an effort to stay connected.

To navigate this, try to listen to the emotions behind her words. Pay attention to the situation she's in, her tone of voice, and any non-verbal cues that can help you understand what's implied but not directly stated.

Recognizing When She's Testing Your Attentiveness

Sometimes, indirect communication is a way for women to test how attentive you are to her needs. If she says something that seems vague or unclear, she might be checking whether you're really listening and picking up on the subtleties of the conversation. This can feel like a small, subtle test of your emotional awareness and your ability to understand her without her needing to spell everything out.

For example, if she says, "It's fine, I'll just do it myself," she's not only hinting at frustration; she might be seeing if you notice her need for help and respond accordingly. If you don't pick up on it, she may feel unheard or unimportant. On the other hand, if you do respond with care and attentiveness, it shows that you're tuned in to her emotional state and willing to act on it.

This type of indirect communication can be a way for women to test how emotionally present you are, and whether you are truly attuned to what's going on beneath the surface. To pass this test, be sure to listen actively, offer help when it's needed, and check in with her feelings regularly.

Conclusion

In this chapter, we've explored the power of **indirect communication** and how it plays a significant role in how women express themselves. By understanding why women often speak indirectly, how to interpret their subtle hints, and recognizing the emotional layers beneath their words, you can communicate with more empathy and insight. The key to mastering this aspect of communication is paying attention to what's being said—and also to what's left unsaid. When you learn to read between the lines, you'll be better equipped to understand her true feelings and needs.

Words that Mean Something Else

In communication, words are more than just words—they can carry layers of meaning that are often unspoken. One of the most important aspects of understanding the language of women is recognizing that certain phrases might not mean exactly what they seem to on the surface. Women often use language in a way that signals deeper emotions, needs, or expectations. By learning to decode these phrases, you can better understand her feelings and respond in a way that shows you are truly listening.

Common Phrases with Hidden Meanings

There are many phrases that women use where the meaning isn't always immediately obvious. These are statements that, on the surface, might seem straightforward, but in reality, they carry hidden emotional layers. Recognizing these phrases and understanding the emotional context behind them can help you avoid misunderstandings and respond with more empathy.

For example, when a woman says, "It's fine," you might assume that everything is okay. But more often than not, "It's fine" actually signals that something isn't fine at all. It's a way of masking frustration or disappointment without starting an argument. When you hear "It's fine," it's a good idea to pay closer attention to her tone of voice, body language, and the overall context. Her use of this phrase is often a subtle cue that something is bothering her, but she may not feel comfortable addressing it directly.

"I'm Fine" as a Signal of Dissatisfaction

The phrase "I'm fine" is one of the most commonly used phrases with hidden meaning. While it may sound like everything is okay, "I'm fine" is often a signal that something is wrong. It's a way of expressing dissatisfaction or frustration without directly saying it. The reason behind this is that many women don't want to create conflict or make the situation worse by confronting their feelings head-on.

When a woman says, "I'm fine," it's a good time to pause and reflect. Is she really fine, or is she trying to avoid conflict by not opening up? This phrase often indicates that she might be upset, hurt, or disappointed, but doesn't want to escalate things. Instead of brushing it off, try asking open-ended questions to gently probe deeper, such as, "You don't seem fine. What's really going on?" Showing that you care enough to ask and listen can help her feel safe to express herself more openly.

What "We Need to Talk" Really Means

Another common phrase with hidden meaning is, "We need to talk." This phrase can create instant anxiety, because it often signals that something serious is going on. When a woman says, "We need to talk," it's typically an indication that there's an issue or concern she wants to discuss, but it doesn't always mean it's a major problem.

However, the fact that she uses this phrase suggests that the conversation will likely involve some level of emotional depth or vulnerability. It's important to approach this conversation with patience and an open mind. Often, "We need to talk" means that she's feeling something—whether it's frustration, sadness, or confusion—and she wants you to understand her perspective. Respond by creating a safe, non-judgmental space for her to express what's on her mind, showing that you're ready to listen and take her feelings seriously.

The Role of "Guilt Talk" and Emotional Triggers

Women sometimes use what we call "guilt talk" to communicate their emotional needs. Guilt talk doesn't always mean that a woman is trying to make you feel bad on purpose; instead, it's often a way of expressing her emotions indirectly or highlighting something she feels is missing or unresolved. Phrases like, "I can't believe I'm always the one doing this," or "No one ever notices how hard I try," may seem like complaints, but they often reflect unmet emotional needs or feelings of being undervalued.

These phrases trigger emotional responses by making you feel guilty or responsible, but the deeper meaning behind them is often that she is seeking recognition or support. She might be hoping that you will notice her efforts and offer help or appreciation without her needing to directly ask for it.

Recognizing guilt talk for what it is—an emotional signal rather than a direct accusation—helps you avoid feeling defensive and instead focus on responding to the need beneath the words. If you hear a phrase like this, try acknowledging her feelings and offering support or validation, such as, "I see you've been working hard. Let me help with that."

How Guilt Is Used to Communicate Emotional Needs

Guilt is often used as a tool for communicating emotional needs. It's not about manipulation but rather a way of signaling to someone that something is missing in the relationship or that emotional needs aren't being fully met. Women may not always feel comfortable directly asking for what they need, especially if they fear it will come across as too demanding or needy. So instead, they may use guilt to gently nudge their partner toward the desired outcome.

For example, if a woman says, "I've been taking care of everything around here," she's likely expressing a need for help and shared responsibility, but she may not want to directly say, "I need you to do more." Instead, she's conveying that she's overwhelmed and needs support, without explicitly asking for it. The key here is recognizing that guilt isn't necessarily about blaming; it's about expressing a deeper emotional need that hasn't been voiced yet.

To respond effectively, don't focus on the guilt aspect or become defensive. Instead, focus on the emotional message she's trying to communicate.

Acknowledge that her needs are valid, and offer a solution that shows you're listening and willing to help.

Understanding the Underlying Requests Hidden Within Statements

Often, the hidden meaning in women's words isn't just about how they feel—it's also about what they want or need from the conversation. When she says something like, "I don't know, I just feel like I'm doing everything," the implied request might be, "Can you help me more?" or "I need more support." Understanding these underlying requests is key to responding in a way that meets her needs.

To do this, you need to pay attention to the emotional tone behind the words. Is she expressing frustration, loneliness, or a desire for attention? Often, what she's saying on the surface isn't the complete picture. Look for the deeper, unspoken request: does she need reassurance, help, understanding, or validation?

By learning to recognize these hidden requests, you can respond more thoughtfully and be more proactive in meeting her needs. Sometimes the best way to understand these requests is by asking for clarity. You might say, "It sounds like you're feeling overwhelmed—how can I help?" or "I hear that you're frustrated. Let's talk about what you need."

Conclusion

In this chapter, we've explored the concept of **words that mean something else** - phrases that carry hidden meanings, emotional cues, and unspoken requests. By learning to recognize these phrases and understand what's really being communicated, you can respond in a way that shows empathy, understanding, and attentiveness. The key is to listen not just to the words, but also to the emotions and needs that lie beneath them. When you master this, you'll be much better equipped to truly understand her and build a deeper, more connected relationship.

Emotional Expression Through Language

One of the most important aspects of understanding the language of women is recognizing how emotions are expressed through words. Women often use a rich emotional vocabulary to communicate how they feel, but the language they use can sometimes be subtle or layered with meaning. By learning to identify the emotional signals behind the words, you can respond more thoughtfully and provide the emotional support she needs. In this chapter, we will explore how women express their emotions through language and how to navigate these expressions with understanding and empathy.

Women's Emotional Vocabulary and What It Signals

Women often have a more expansive emotional vocabulary than men, and they tend to use words that reflect a wide range of feelings. When a woman describes how she's feeling, the words she chooses can give you insight into her emotional state. For example, a woman might use terms like "frustrated," "disappointed," "hurt," or "overwhelmed," each of which carries its own specific emotional weight.

Understanding these words helps you see beyond the surface and understand what's truly going on emotionally. For instance, when a woman says she's "frustrated," it might not only mean that something isn't going the way she wants, but also that she feels powerless or stuck in a situation. On the other hand, if she says she's "disappointed," it signals that her expectations were unmet, and she might feel let down or neglected.

Recognizing these differences allows you to respond appropriately. When she says she's "hurt," for instance, it's important to acknowledge her feelings with empathy, rather than immediately trying to fix the situation. By paying attention to the specific emotions she expresses, you show that you understand and care about what she's going through.

Differentiating Between Anger, Frustration, and Disappointment

One challenge in understanding emotional expression through language is distinguishing between similar emotions, such as anger, frustration, and disappointment. These feelings can overlap and often get expressed in similar ways, but each has its own unique meaning and emotional impact.

- **Anger** tends to be a more intense, outwardly expressed emotion. It may come with words like "mad," "furious," or "enraged." When a woman is angry, she might express it more directly and may even raise her voice. Anger often arises from a perceived injustice or violation of boundaries.

- **Frustration** is a feeling of being blocked or unable to achieve a goal, often accompanied by irritation. Words like "annoyed," "fed up," or "stuck" might be used. Frustration can be less intense than anger but still signals a desire for things to change.

- **Disappointment** signals a sense of unmet expectations and is often more subtle. When a woman says she's "disappointed," it indicates that her hopes or desires were not fulfilled, and she feels let down. Disappointment can often be expressed quietly, with phrases like "I thought things would be different."

Understanding these emotional distinctions helps you respond appropriately. For instance, if she's angry, she may need space to vent and cool down, while frustration might require a more solution-oriented approach. Disappointment, however, often needs a comforting, reassuring response to help her feel heard and understood.

Understanding the Need for Empathy vs. Solutions

One of the most common communication challenges between men and women revolves around the difference between seeking empathy and seeking solutions. Women often want to feel heard and understood when they express their emotions, while men might instinctively try to solve the problem.

If a woman says she's upset, she might not be looking for a solution right away. Instead, she might just want someone to listen and empathize with her feelings. For example, if she's frustrated at work, she may not need you to tell her how to fix the situation. Instead, she might just want you to say something like, "I can see how that would be really stressful" or "That sounds really tough."

On the other hand, if she is asking for advice or a solution, she might directly say, "What should I do?" or "Do you think I should try this?" Knowing the difference between when she needs empathy and when she needs a solution is key to providing the right response. Sometimes, just listening and validating her feelings can go a long way, while other times, offering a thoughtful suggestion can help her feel supported and guided.

How Emotional Needs Are Conveyed Through Words

Women often use language to convey their emotional needs without directly stating them. Phrases like "I don't know what I'd do without you" or "I wish I had someone to talk to" might not always be about the immediate situation but can signal a deeper emotional need for connection, reassurance, or support.

When women use phrases like this, they're expressing a longing for emotional support, understanding, or validation. Recognizing these needs allows you to respond more sensitively. For example, instead of simply acknowledging the words, try to understand the underlying emotional need: she might be feeling isolated, overwhelmed, or unappreciated. By responding with empathy, like "I'm here for you" or "You don't have to go through this alone," you can provide the emotional support she's asking for.

Understanding these subtle cues also helps you avoid misunderstandings. If a woman says, "I'm fine," but her tone suggests otherwise, she may be conveying a need for emotional connection or reassurance. Responding with, "It seems like something's bothering you—want to talk about it?" shows you're tuned into her emotional needs and willing to engage in a meaningful conversation.

Identifying When She's Seeking Reassurance

Sometimes, women use language to seek reassurance, particularly when they're feeling uncertain or vulnerable. Phrases like "Do you still love me?" or "Am I doing okay?" are common ways of expressing a need for reassurance. These words are signals that she's seeking affirmation, comfort, or validation about something she's feeling unsure about.

When a woman asks for reassurance, she's often looking for emotional security. She may be experiencing self-doubt or worrying about the stability of the relationship. It's important to recognize these cues and respond in a way that reassures her, such as saying, "Of course, I love you," or "You're doing great, and I'm proud of you."

Providing reassurance isn't about solving the problem, but about offering emotional support and making her feel secure and valued. Recognizing when she needs reassurance and offering it in a calm, steady manner can help her feel more emotionally grounded.

Recognizing When She's Expressing Vulnerability

Vulnerability is a powerful part of emotional expression, and women often use language to express vulnerability, whether they're consciously aware of it or not. Phrases like "I don't know what to do," "I'm scared," or "I feel lost" are indications that she's opening up and showing her more vulnerable side. Vulnerability is often a sign of trust—it's a way of saying, "I'm letting my guard down, and I need you to be there for me."

When you hear these kinds of statements, it's important to respond with empathy and understanding, rather than offering solutions right away. Vulnerability requires care, support, and emotional connection. Instead of trying to fix the problem, offer her a listening ear and let her know that it's okay to feel the way she does. Saying something like, "I understand, and I'm here for you" can be incredibly comforting.

By recognizing vulnerability in her language, you show that you value her trust and are willing to be emotionally present. This strengthens the bond between you and helps her feel safe and supported.

Conclusion

In this section, we've explored how **emotions are expressed through language**, and how women often use specific words and phrases to signal their emotional states and needs. By understanding the emotional vocabulary, recognizing the difference between anger, frustration, and disappointment, and responding to her needs for empathy, reassurance, and support, you can deepen your emotional connection and improve your communication. By listening carefully and responding with understanding, you create a safe space for her to express her feelings and needs openly.

3

Understanding Unspoken Signals

Mastering the Art of Listening

Listening is one of the most powerful tools you have in understanding someone, especially when it comes to the language of women. However, there's a big difference between hearing and truly listening. To hear is a passive action; to listen is active, intentional, and empathetic. In this chapter, we will explore how you can master the art of listening—how to go beyond simply hearing the words, and instead, truly understand the emotions, needs, and intentions behind them.

The Difference Between Hearing and Truly Listening

At its core, hearing is just the physical process of perceiving sound. You might hear someone speaking, but it doesn't necessarily mean you're paying attention or absorbing the message. Truly listening, on the other hand, requires focus, intention, and engagement. When you listen actively, you're not just hearing words—you're connecting with the speaker on a deeper level, understanding their emotions, and empathizing with their experience.

Many men struggle with this distinction, particularly when a woman is expressing frustration, sadness, or other emotions. Men often focus on the words alone, looking for a "solution" or a "fix," when what she really needs is someone to listen, understand, and validate her feelings. Active listening is about giving her your full attention, not just to her words, but to her emotional state and body language as well. This requires patience and presence.

When you listen actively, you communicate that you value her thoughts and feelings. You show her that her voice matters, and that you're willing to invest in truly understanding what she is trying to communicate. This goes a long way in building trust, empathy, and connection.

Techniques to Focus on Her Emotional State, Not Just Her Words

One of the key aspects of active listening is recognizing that the true meaning of her words often lies in the emotions behind them. Women tend to express their feelings more openly, and their words can sometimes carry emotional weight that may not be immediately obvious.

To truly listen, you need to focus on her emotional state, not just what she's saying. Notice how she's saying it—the tone of her voice, the pace of her speech, her facial expressions, and her body language. Is she speaking quickly or slowly? Does her voice tremble or seem steady? These physical cues will give you a clearer understanding of how she's feeling.

For example, if she's talking about something that seems minor to you but she sounds upset or frustrated, it's likely that the situation is triggering deeper emotions. Perhaps there's more to the story than what's on the surface. Instead of dismissing the emotion or jumping to conclusions, take a moment to acknowledge her feelings. You could say, "I can tell this is really bothering you. Do you want to talk about it?"

This approach helps you connect with her on a deeper level, and it shows her that you're listening not just to the words, but to the emotions and needs behind them.

The Role of Silence in Communication

Silence is often an overlooked but incredibly powerful tool in communication. Sometimes, the most meaningful moments in a conversation happen during pauses. Silence gives both parties time to reflect, process, and think before responding. It allows the speaker to gather her thoughts and helps the listener fully absorb what's being said.

Many people, particularly in fast-paced conversations, feel compelled to fill every silence with words, either to clarify a point or to avoid discomfort.

However, silence doesn't have to be awkward or uncomfortable—it can be an invitation for deeper connection. When a woman is speaking and then pauses, don't rush in to fill the space. Instead, use this moment to really absorb what she's shared and how it made you feel.

By allowing the silence to exist, you give her the space to share more if she chooses. She may reveal more details or express emotions she didn't initially put into words. And sometimes, silence itself may indicate that she needs comfort, but isn't sure how to express it yet.

Interpreting What's Not Being Said

While listening to someone's words is important, truly understanding her means paying attention to what's not being said. Sometimes, women express emotions, thoughts, or needs indirectly or leave certain things unspoken. These unspoken cues can carry just as much significance as the words she uses.

Pay attention to any non-verbal communication that might be revealing deeper emotions or concerns. For example, if she says, "I'm just tired," but her tone sounds resigned or defeated, this could be a sign that she's not just physically tired, but emotionally drained. Or, if she talks about a problem without offering a clear solution, she might be seeking support or validation rather than a quick fix.

Often, the most important part of communication happens in the moments between words—through body language, pauses, and unspoken thoughts. By listening for these subtle signals, you show that you care not just about the conversation, but about her emotional experience as a whole.

When Silence Is an Invitation for Deeper Connection

Sometimes, silence isn't a sign of discomfort, but a sign that she's opening up to you on a deeper level. When a woman is quiet, especially after sharing something vulnerable or emotional, it can be an invitation for you to connect more deeply and support her without the need for immediate verbal response.

In these moments, avoid trying to fill the silence with words. Instead, sit with her in the quiet and let her know that you're there. This simple act of presence can speak volumes. Sometimes, she may be processing her emotions and doesn't know how to express them yet. By remaining silent and giving her the space to reflect, you allow her the room to open up in her own time.

If she has shared something deeply personal or emotional, and there is a pause afterward, you could say, "I'm here with you," or "Take your time, I'm listening." This lets her know that you're fully present and that you care about her experience. Sometimes, that silence becomes a space for her to trust you more deeply, knowing that you're not rushing her to say more than she's ready to.

Conclusion

Mastering the art of listening isn't just about hearing words—it's about understanding the emotions, intentions, and needs behind those words. By focusing on her emotional state, reading between the lines, and recognizing the power of silence, you can foster deeper connection, trust, and empathy. True listening requires patience, attention, and care, but it is one of the most powerful ways to build understanding and strengthen your relationship. When you listen with your heart, you give her the space to truly be heard, and that is one of the most meaningful gifts you can offer.

Reading Between the Lines of Her Actions

While words are powerful tools of communication, often it's her actions that speak the loudest. What she does—how she behaves, interacts, or even withdraws—can reveal much more about her feelings, needs, and state of mind than what she says. In this chapter, we will explore how to read between the lines of her actions, recognizing the deeper emotional meaning behind her behavior and understanding what's being communicated without words.

How Her Behavior Communicates What Words Do Not

Actions can sometimes express feelings that words simply cannot. While words can be carefully chosen and may be influenced by social expectations or fear of vulnerability, actions tend to be more instinctual. They offer a raw and honest reflection of what someone truly feels.

For example, if a woman says, "I'm fine," but her actions suggest otherwise—maybe she pulls away emotionally, avoids eye contact, or becomes quiet—these behaviors may indicate that something is wrong. Her actions reveal that she is not truly "fine," even though her words say otherwise. Recognizing these discrepancies allows you to connect with her on a deeper level, understanding that sometimes her behavior is a more accurate indicator of her emotional state than the words she chooses.

When a woman is upset but doesn't say anything, her actions might give you clues about how she's feeling. She might withdraw from physical affection, or perhaps she'll become more distant emotionally. These actions may be her way of signalling that she needs space, is hurt, or is dealing with something that she doesn't yet feel ready to express in words.

Recognizing the Connection Between Actions and Feelings

There is a strong connection between a person's actions and their feelings. A woman's actions can act as a direct reflection of her emotional state. For instance, if she's upset but doesn't verbalize it, she might still express her feelings through physical cues, such as crossing her arms, avoiding touch, or becoming more distant. Alternatively, if she's feeling loved and cared for, her behavior may be warm, affectionate, and open.

Recognizing this connection helps you interpret what's really going on. If you see her behaving in ways that indicate discomfort or emotional withdrawal, it might not be because of something you did wrong. Instead, it could indicate that she's dealing with stress, insecurity, or other emotions that she may not be ready to talk about. The key is to observe her behavior and respond with understanding, rather than rushing to judgment based on words alone.

One example of this is when a woman goes out of her way to do something thoughtful for you, like preparing a meal or doing something special. This action is often a sign of care and affection—something she might not always express directly with words, but her actions speak volumes. Similarly, if she withdraws into herself or becomes more distant, this could indicate that something in the relationship or in her life is bothering her, even if she hasn't yet spoken about it.

The Importance of Consistency Between Words and Actions

When a woman's actions align with her words, it builds trust and clarity in the relationship. Consistency between what she says and what she does creates a sense of reliability and transparency. However, when there is a disconnect between her words and actions, it can lead to confusion or even frustration.

For example, if she says she wants to spend time with you but repeatedly cancels plans, her words and actions don't match. This inconsistency may leave you wondering whether she is genuinely interested or if there's something more going on beneath the surface. In these cases, it's important to approach the situation with patience and curiosity. Instead of immediately jumping to conclusions, consider asking her gently about her actions to better understand the reasons behind them.

At the same time, if her actions consistently reflect her words—like when she shows up when she says she will, or expresses affection in ways that match her verbal communication—it strengthens the connection between you and makes her feel heard and valued. When there is alignment between what is said and what is done, trust and intimacy can grow.

Subtle Clues in Her Routines and Habits

Her daily routines and habits can also provide valuable clues about her emotional state and needs. The way she spends her time, organizes her space, or interacts with her environment can reveal a lot about how she's feeling.

For example, if she consistently prioritizes self-care activities like exercising, journaling, or spending quiet time alone, this could indicate a need for emotional balance and personal space. It may signal that she's recharging or processing emotions and that she values taking care of herself. On the other hand, if she's constantly busy with work or taking care of others and neglecting her own needs, it could be a sign that she's overwhelmed or struggling with burnout.

Subtle clues in her routines might also indicate her emotional needs in the relationship. If she initiates regular check-ins or sets aside time for intimacy and connection, it could reflect her desire for emotional closeness and attention. If she's distant or avoids certain activities or conversations, it might be a signal that she's feeling neglected or disconnected.

How Daily Behaviors Can Reveal Emotional Needs

Often, women's emotional needs are expressed through their daily behaviors, even if they're not explicitly verbalized. For example, if she shows affection through small gestures—like making sure your favorite food is in the fridge or sending you a thoughtful message—it reflects her emotional investment in the relationship. These behaviors signal that she wants to nurture the bond and ensure you feel loved and appreciated.

Alternatively, if she becomes more withdrawn, avoids physical touch, or seems disinterested in spending time with you, it might suggest that she needs more attention or emotional reassurance. In these cases, her actions are signaling that there may be an unmet emotional need, whether it's a desire for closeness, support, or understanding.

Taking note of these behaviors can help you understand what she needs emotionally, even if she's not expressing it in words. By responding to these signals with empathy and care, you show her that you are paying attention to her emotional well-being and that you're there to meet her needs.

The Impact of Personal Space and Gestures on Her Comfort Level

Another important aspect of understanding her actions is recognizing how personal space and gestures affect her comfort level. Physical gestures and proximity can communicate a great deal about her feelings and boundaries. For instance, if she moves closer to you, leans in during conversation, or initiates touch, it generally indicates that she feels comfortable and emotionally safe with you. These gestures are signs of affection and connection.

However, if she pulls away, avoids touch, or maintains a certain physical distance, it might suggest that she's feeling emotionally guarded, stressed, or even overwhelmed. Personal space is a vital component of comfort in any relationship, and respecting her boundaries—whether physical or emotional—can foster a sense of trust and safety.

It's also important to recognize that her comfort level may change depending on the situation. If she's upset or stressed, she might need more space to process her emotions. On the other hand, if she's feeling emotionally open or affectionate, she may seek more closeness.

Conclusion

In this chapter, we've explored how **her actions can communicate what words often cannot**. By observing her behavior, you gain insight into her emotional state and needs, even when she doesn't explicitly express them. Whether it's through subtle routines, gestures, or the consistency between words and actions, recognizing the emotional messages behind her behavior allows you to connect more deeply and respond in ways that nurture the relationship. Understanding the powerful language of actions is key to building a stronger, more empathetic connection.

Understanding Emotional Timing

When it comes to communicating effectively, **timing** is just as important as the words you choose. Emotions are complex, and the right moment can make all the difference in how a conversation unfolds. Understanding emotional timing means knowing when to approach her, when to give her space, and when to dive into a deeper conversation. In this chapter, we'll explore how timing influences communication, and how you can become more attuned to her emotional state to ensure that meaningful conversations happen when they matter most.

Recognizing When to Approach the Conversation

One of the most important skills in any relationship is knowing **when to approach a conversation**. If you try to talk to her when she's upset, distracted, or emotionally overwhelmed, the chances of a productive conversation are slim. If she's feeling emotional, she may not be ready to engage in meaningful dialogue just yet. In fact, forcing the conversation could create more tension or make her shut down.

To recognize when it's the right time to talk, pay attention to her emotional cues. Does she seem calm and receptive, or is she visibly frustrated or withdrawn? If she's upset, it might be a good idea to give her time to cool down before addressing sensitive topics. This doesn't mean avoiding the conversation entirely—it just means being mindful of her emotional state and waiting until she's in a more open, balanced frame of mind.

Sometimes, the best way to approach a conversation is simply by asking, "Is now a good time to talk?" This shows her that you respect her emotional boundaries and that you're not trying to force an uncomfortable conversation. By being mindful of when she's ready, you increase the chances of the conversation being productive and respectful.

Picking the Right Moment for Meaningful Dialogue

Knowing when to have a meaningful conversation is just as important as what you say. The environment and timing can greatly impact how well the conversation goes. For example, if you're at a family gathering or she's in the middle of something stressful, it's probably not the best time to talk about something important. The right moment is when both of you are emotionally ready and in a calm, distraction-free setting.

Choose a moment when she's not overwhelmed by other commitments, emotions, or external stressors. A quiet evening at home or a peaceful walk together can provide the perfect backdrop for a deep, meaningful conversation. During these moments, both of you are more likely to be receptive, open, and emotionally available to each other.

Sometimes, the right moment may not be obvious, but by staying tuned to her emotional state, you can sense when she's more open to discussing things that matter. If she seems relaxed, engaged, and present, that's often the best time to have a conversation that requires vulnerability or depth.

How Emotions Influence Her Openness to Communication

Emotions play a central role in her ability to communicate openly. When a woman is feeling **stressed, anxious, or overwhelmed**, her capacity to engage in thoughtful, meaningful dialogue may be limited. In contrast, when she's feeling **secure, calm, and emotionally supported**, she's more likely to open up and engage in honest conversation.

If she's going through something emotionally challenging—whether it's related to work, family, or personal stress—she may not be ready to talk about relationship matters or deeper emotional issues. Recognizing when she's emotionally drained or dealing with heavy feelings helps you avoid pushing her into a conversation she's not ready for.

On the flip side, if she's in a positive emotional space, expressing affection, or feeling understood, this could be a great time to discuss important topics or even bring up any concerns. Timing your approach according to her emotional state shows that you're paying attention and respect her emotional needs.

Learning to Give Her Space When Needed

Space is just as crucial as time spent together in a relationship. Sometimes, giving her physical or emotional space is the best way to support her. If she's feeling overwhelmed or needs time to process her thoughts, stepping back and allowing her to have that space can give her the time to reflect and find clarity.

It's important to recognize when she needs space, and this isn't always a sign of disinterest or withdrawal. She may need time alone to recharge, to think things through, or to manage her emotions. Pushing for a conversation when she's asking for space can create more tension and frustration.

When you respect her need for space, it shows maturity and understanding. Instead of pressuring her, simply say something like, "I understand you need some time. Let me know when you're ready to talk." This communicates that you're not ignoring the issue but that you care enough to give her the room she needs to be emotionally ready.

Understanding the Need for Reflection Before Deep Talks

Sometimes, **reflection** is necessary before jumping into a deep conversation. After an emotional or stressful event, both of you may need time to process your feelings before discussing them openly. This time for reflection allows emotions to settle, which can lead to a more productive and thoughtful discussion.

If a woman is upset or confused about something, she may need a little time to sort through her thoughts and understand how she feels. Forcing an immediate conversation can lead to miscommunication or unnecessary conflict. Instead, allow her the time to reflect, and when she's ready, she will be more prepared to engage in a meaningful, constructive dialogue.

Giving space for reflection isn't about avoiding the conversation—it's about creating the conditions where both of you can express yourselves calmly and clearly. By acknowledging her need for reflection, you show that you care about her emotional well-being and that you're willing to wait for the right moment to talk.

How Timing Impacts the Success of a Conversation

Timing is a key factor in how successful a conversation will be. If you approach a conversation too soon, before she's emotionally ready, or at a time when she's distracted, it can lead to misunderstandings, frustration, or even avoidance. Conversely, if you wait for the right time—when she's calm, receptive, and ready to engage—the conversation is more likely to be productive, meaningful, and respectful.

Think of timing like planting a seed. If you try to plant it in rocky, dry soil, it won't grow. But if you wait for the right moment—when the conditions are right—the seed can thrive. Similarly, a conversation needs the right emotional and environmental conditions to flourish.

In relationships, emotional timing isn't about waiting for perfection—it's about being aware of each other's emotional needs and respecting when the time is right for both of you to talk. When you understand the emotional rhythms of your relationship and approach conversations with care and timing, the success of those conversations will follow naturally.

Conclusion

Mastering **emotional timing** is essential for deepening your connection and understanding. By recognizing when to approach a conversation, picking the right moments for dialogue, respecting the need for space, and allowing time for reflection, you can ensure that your conversations are not only more effective but also more compassionate. With the right timing, your discussions will be more productive, and your relationship will grow stronger as a result.

4

Building Lasting Connections

Developing Empathy and Emotional Intelligence

In any relationship, **empathy** and **emotional intelligence** are the keys to truly understanding and connecting with each other. These qualities allow you to not only recognize your partner's emotions but also respond to them in a way that strengthens your bond. By tuning into her emotional world, validating her feelings, and becoming more emotionally aware, you can deepen your connection and create a more supportive, understanding relationship.

How to Tune Into Her Emotional World

Tuning into her emotional world starts with **being present**—not just physically, but emotionally. Pay attention to how she feels, not just what she says. Emotions often run deeper than words, and the key to understanding her is to listen beyond the surface. Does she seem happy, anxious, frustrated, or tired? Often, emotions can be conveyed through body language, facial expressions, and tone of voice, even if she doesn't directly say how she feels.

For example, when she's feeling stressed, she might be quieter, more withdrawn, or even fidgeting. Recognizing these signs shows that you're tuned into her emotional state. Being mindful of these subtle cues allows you to respond in a way that acknowledges her feelings, offering comfort or support as needed.

Understanding her emotional world requires patience and practice. It means learning to read her moods and signals and reacting with care, not rushing to fix or minimize her feelings. Simply being aware of her emotional shifts allows you to better meet her needs and create a deeper emotional connection.

Understanding the Importance of Validating Her Feelings

One of the most powerful ways to show empathy is by **validating her feelings**. This doesn't mean you always have to agree with her emotions, but it's about acknowledging them as real and important. When you validate her feelings, you show that you respect her emotional experience, even if it's different from your own.

For example, if she's upset, instead of immediately trying to fix the problem, you might say, "I can see that this is really bothering you," or "It makes sense that you're feeling this way." Validation helps her feel heard, understood, and supported. It signals that her emotions are valid and that her perspective matters.

When you validate her feelings, you open the door for her to express herself more openly. It builds trust and helps create a safe space for vulnerability. This act of empathy fosters emotional intimacy and makes her feel more connected to you.

Recognizing Emotional Cues That Guide Responses

Part of developing emotional intelligence is learning to **recognize emotional cues** that guide your response. Emotions are often expressed in subtle ways, such as through body language, tone of voice, or facial expressions. When you pick up on these cues, you can tailor your responses to what she needs at the moment.

For example, if she's visibly upset but hasn't said much, you might notice her posture is closed, or she's avoiding eye contact. These are emotional cues that tell you she might need space or support. If she's speaking in a soft or distant tone, it could be a sign that she's feeling emotionally distant or not ready to talk.

In these situations, it's important to listen closely and pay attention to what she's conveying non-verbally. Responding to these cues with patience and understanding helps to create a more emotionally intelligent exchange. Whether she needs a listening ear or a comforting touch, recognizing these signals lets you meet her where she is emotionally.

The Role of Emotional Intelligence in Relationships

Emotional intelligence (EQ) is the ability to recognize, understand, and manage emotions—both your own and others'. In relationships, EQ plays a vital role in navigating challenges, building empathy, and communicating effectively. A high level of emotional intelligence helps you to respond to your partner's emotional needs with care and wisdom.

When you have emotional intelligence, you're more likely to remain calm in tense situations, manage your own emotions, and empathize with her feelings. Instead of reacting impulsively or defensively, you can pause, understand her perspective, and respond in a way that fosters connection.

For example, if you're in a disagreement, emotional intelligence allows you to see things from her point of view and remain open to finding a solution. It helps you communicate with respect, even in difficult conversations, and prevents emotions from escalating into arguments. The more you develop your emotional intelligence, the more resilient your relationship will be.

Identifying Emotional Triggers for Both Partners

Every person has **emotional triggers**—things that provoke strong emotional reactions. These triggers can be linked to past experiences, insecurities, or specific situations. By identifying each other's emotional triggers, you can learn to avoid or handle them more effectively, preventing unnecessary conflict and frustration.

For example, if she has a trigger related to feeling ignored or unheard, she might become defensive or withdraw when she feels you're not paying attention. Recognizing this pattern gives you the opportunity to be more attentive and responsive to her needs. On the other hand, you may have your own emotional triggers, such as feeling criticized or disrespected.

Identifying these triggers allows both of you to communicate more thoughtfully, avoiding situations that may lead to emotional discomfort.

Once you both understand each other's triggers, you can work together to minimize them and create a healthier emotional environment. Emotional awareness not only helps you understand how to react in the moment but also builds a foundation for deeper emotional connection and mutual support.

Using Emotional Awareness to Strengthen Bonds

Ultimately, **emotional awareness** is about being present, listening with empathy, and responding thoughtfully. When both partners are emotionally aware, they can respond to each other's needs in a compassionate way, strengthening the bond between them. This emotional intelligence fosters trust, respect, and a deeper sense of connection.

For example, when you recognize her emotional state and respond with empathy, you show that you care about her feelings and are there to support her. Similarly, when she understands your emotions and respects your emotional needs, it creates a sense of partnership and understanding. Together, you can navigate challenges more smoothly, knowing that you are emotionally in tune with one another.

Emotional awareness strengthens bonds by creating an atmosphere of mutual respect and trust. When you both feel understood and supported, the relationship flourishes. By investing in emotional intelligence and empathy, you create a safe space where both partners can grow, communicate openly, and connect on a deeper emotional level.

In this chapter, we've explored how **developing empathy and emotional intelligence** can transform your relationship. By tuning into her emotional world, validating her feelings, recognizing emotional cues, and understanding triggers, you create a foundation of trust and respect. Emotional intelligence is essential in fostering a connection that's not only based on love but also on mutual understanding and emotional awareness. When both partners develop these skills, the relationship becomes stronger, more resilient, and more emotionally fulfilling.

Using Your New Skills in Everyday Communication

Now that you've developed a deeper understanding of the language of women and honed your emotional intelligence, it's time to put these skills to work in your daily conversations. Effective communication isn't just about what you say—it's about how you listen, how you respond, and how you make her feel heard and understood. By using your new skills in everyday communication, you can strengthen your relationship, build rapport, and create a deeper connection with her.

Building Rapport Through Active Listening and Empathy

The foundation of any great conversation is **active listening**. It's more than just hearing words—it's about fully focusing on her and making her feel like the center of your attention. Active listening means you're not just waiting for your turn to speak, but you're really taking in what she's saying, both verbally and non-verbally.

When you practice active listening, you signal to her that her thoughts, feelings, and concerns matter to you. This creates **rapport** and makes her feel valued. Empathy enhances this further. It's not just about understanding her words; it's about understanding her emotions behind the words. Show her that you truly get how she feels. A simple, "I understand why you're upset," can go a long way in reinforcing your connection.

Tip: Make eye contact, nod occasionally, and show you're engaged. These small gestures make a big difference in how she feels during the conversation.

Techniques to Make Her Feel Heard and Understood

Sometimes, what matters most to her is not just the solution to a problem, but the feeling of being **heard and understood**. To make her feel truly listened to, try these techniques:

- **Paraphrasing:** After she shares something, repeat it back to her in your own words. For example, "So, you're saying that you felt left out when I didn't ask for your opinion on that decision. I can see how that would upset you." This shows her that you're not just hearing her, but actively processing what she's saying.

- **Validation:** Instead of immediately offering advice, acknowledge her feelings. "I understand why you would feel that way," or "That must have been frustrating for you." These responses show that you respect her emotional experience.
- **Minimal Encouragers:** Use short phrases or sounds like "I see," "Go on," or "That makes sense." These encourage her to continue speaking and show that you're interested in what she has to say.

How to Ask the Right Questions to Deepen Understanding

Asking the right questions is crucial in deepening your understanding of her thoughts and feelings. Rather than assuming, ask open-ended questions that invite her to share more.

- **Open-Ended Questions:** Instead of asking yes or no questions, try, "How did that make you feel?" or "What do you think would help in this situation?" These questions encourage her to express herself more fully.
- **Clarifying Questions:** If you're not sure about something she said, ask for clarification. For example, "Can you explain what you meant when you said...?" This shows that you care about understanding her completely.
- **Reflective Questions:** After she's shared her thoughts, reflect back what she said and ask for more. "It sounds like you're saying you felt unsupported. Is that right? What can I do to change that?"

By asking these kinds of questions, you demonstrate curiosity about her experience, which fosters a deeper level of connection and understanding.

Applying Non-Verbal Communication Techniques

Much of communication happens **non-verbally**. What you do with your body, your eyes, and even your tone of voice can say just as much, if not more, than the words you use. **Non-verbal communication** helps reinforce the emotional message you're trying to convey.

Here are some tips for using non-verbal communication to enhance your connection:

- **Maintain open body language**: Keep your posture open and relaxed. Avoid crossing your arms or turning away, as these can signal disinterest or defensiveness.
- **Use facial expressions**: Smiling, nodding, or showing empathy through facial expressions makes you appear more approachable and connected.
- **Lean in slightly**: Leaning in during conversation shows you're interested and engaged in what she's saying.
- **Match her energy**: If she's speaking quietly and thoughtfully, matching that tone can help you connect. If she's animated and excited, adjusting your energy to reflect that can reinforce rapport.

Reinforcing Connection with Appropriate Body Language

Body language is one of the most powerful tools for **reinforcing emotional connection**. The right gestures and movements can help deepen your bond and show her that you care.

- **Touch**: A gentle touch on the arm or a comforting hug can communicate empathy and understanding, especially when words are insufficient.
- **Mirroring**: Subtly mirroring her posture or movements can make her feel more comfortable and connected to you. For example, if she crosses her legs, you might cross yours. It's a subtle way to show empathy and establish rapport.
- **Eye contact**: Maintaining soft eye contact shows attentiveness and interest. However, be careful not to stare too intensely, as this could make her feel uncomfortable.

How Gestures and Tone Amplify Empathy in Conversations

Your **tone** and **gestures** are powerful tools in expressing empathy. The tone of your voice can carry as much emotional weight as the words you speak. For example, a calm, warm tone can reassure her that you care, while a sharp or harsh tone may make her feel dismissed or unheard.

Gestures also play an important role in reinforcing the emotional content of a conversation. Simple things like gently touching her hand, leaning in to show interest, or even maintaining good posture convey that you are engaged and emotionally available. These non-verbal cues amplify the message of empathy, making her feel safe and supported.

Conclusion

In everyday communication, the combination of **active listening**, **empathy**, and **non-verbal cues** can make all the difference in how well you understand and connect with her. By tuning into her emotions, asking the right questions, and using body language that reinforces empathy, you build a deeper, more meaningful connection. Every conversation is an opportunity to strengthen the bond you share, and with these skills, you can ensure that your relationship grows through better understanding and communication.

Navigating Conflicts with Better Communication

Conflicts are a natural part of any relationship, but how you handle them can make all the difference in your connection. **Effective communication** during disagreements is not about winning or losing—it's about turning these moments into opportunities for deeper understanding, connection, and growth. When you learn to approach conflicts with patience, empathy, and clear communication, you not only resolve issues more effectively but also strengthen the bond you share.

Turning Disagreements into Opportunities for Connection

Disagreements don't have to drive a wedge between you. In fact, when handled well, conflicts can become an **opportunity for connection**. The key is to approach them with the mindset that you both want to reach a mutual understanding, rather than focusing on who is right or wrong.

Start by remembering that it's not you versus her—it's both of you versus the issue. Approach the disagreement as a team, focused on solving the problem together. By showing empathy and actively listening, you can create a space where both of you feel heard and valued.

For example, if you disagree about something important, try saying, "I can see why you feel that way, and I want to understand more about your perspective." This approach invites her to share her thoughts while showing that you respect her viewpoint. This shift from confrontation to collaboration can transform a potential argument into a productive conversation that brings you closer.

Using Understanding of Her Emotional Needs to Resolve Conflict

Understanding her **emotional needs** is essential when navigating conflict. Women often approach disagreements not just from a logical perspective, but from an emotional one. Knowing what she needs emotionally during a conflict can help you respond in ways that defuse tension and show her that you care.

For example, if she's upset, she may need reassurance or validation rather than a solution right away. A simple statement like, "I understand this is really bothering you, and I want to support you through this," can go a long way in calming her down and making her feel understood.

By acknowledging her emotional state, you create a space for her to feel heard and secure. This emotional understanding opens the door for both of you to work through the issue together, rather than letting emotions escalate the conflict further.

How to Maintain Calm and Control in Heated Moments

During heated moments, it's easy to get caught up in the emotions of the situation. However, maintaining **calm and control** is essential to ensuring the conversation stays productive and respectful. When you stay calm, it not only helps you think more clearly, but it also encourages her to remain composed, which helps keep the conversation on track.

To maintain control in the moment:

- **Take a deep breath** and pause before responding. This gives you a moment to collect your thoughts and choose a response that is calm and constructive.
- **Avoid raising your voice** or using aggressive body language. Instead, maintain a soft tone and keep your posture open and inviting.
- **Stay focused on the issue**, not personal attacks. Stick to talking about the problem at hand, rather than bringing up past mistakes or frustrations. For instance, say, "I think we're having trouble agreeing on this issue," instead of "You always do this."

By staying calm, you show maturity and emotional control, which can help de-escalate the situation and make it easier for her to do the same.

The Importance of Compromise and Clear Communication

In any relationship, **compromise** is key. Both of you have different perspectives, and the goal isn't to "win," but to find a middle ground that works for both of you. Effective communication helps you clearly express your needs, listen to hers, and find a way to meet somewhere in the middle.

For example, if you're debating how to spend your free time, instead of insisting on your own preference, you might say, "I'd love to do X, but I also understand that you prefer Y. How about we try to find a way to do both?" This approach opens the door for collaboration and mutual respect.

Clear communication also involves **speaking up about your own needs** while being considerate of hers. For instance, if you need some alone time after a stressful day, communicate that gently: "I feel like I need a bit of space to recharge, but I also want to make sure we spend time together. How can we make that work?" By being clear and respectful, you can address your needs without dismissing hers.

How to Express Your Own Needs While Understanding Hers

During conflict, it's easy to focus only on how the situation affects you. However, it's just as important to **express your own needs** while being mindful of hers. Healthy relationships thrive on mutual understanding, so it's essential that both partners feel comfortable sharing what they need without fear of judgment or rejection.

When expressing your needs, use **"I" statements** to avoid sounding accusatory. For example, "I feel overwhelmed when we argue, and I need some time to think before we continue the conversation." This way, you're focusing on your own experience rather than blaming her for the situation.

At the same time, ensure you understand her needs. Ask open-ended questions like, "What do you need from me right now?" or "How can I best support you in this situation?" This shows that you're committed to finding a solution that works for both of you, rather than just asserting your own desires.

Learning When to Agree to Disagree

Not every disagreement will end in full agreement, and that's okay. Sometimes, the best way forward is to **agree to disagree**. You both may have different views on a topic, but that doesn't mean the relationship is at risk.

Recognizing when it's time to let go of a disagreement can save both of you from unnecessary tension. For example, if a topic is unlikely to be resolved at the moment, you might say, "I see that we're not going to agree on this right now, but I respect your perspective, and I'm glad we could talk about it." By acknowledging your differences without forcing a resolution, you allow the conversation to end on a positive note, maintaining respect for each other's opinions.

Conclusion

In this chapter, we've explored how **effective communication** can help you navigate conflicts with confidence and empathy. By turning disagreements into opportunities for connection, using your understanding of her emotional needs, maintaining calm, and practicing compromise, you can resolve conflicts in a way that strengthens your bond. Remember, communication is not just about talking—it's about truly understanding and respecting each other's perspectives, even when you don't see eye to eye.

5

Understanding Unspoken Signals

A Learning Journey About Communication

Throughout my career as a communication expert, I've had the privilege of working with countless individuals and couples to improve their communication skills. But it wasn't until I started deeply focusing on the **language of women** that I truly began to understand how intricate and powerful this communication style can be. It's one thing to understand communication theory or to help others navigate difficult conversations, but it's something entirely different to immerse yourself in the nuances of gendered communication—specifically, the way women express themselves emotionally and verbally.

Looking back on my journey, I can pinpoint a few key moments that helped me truly grasp the complexities of women's language and how those lessons shaped my understanding of communication. Let me share some of the insights I've learned along the way, and how these lessons have transformed my approach to relationships, both personal and professional.

A Humbling Beginning: Misunderstanding Her Emotions

When I first started working as a communication expert, I thought I had a strong grasp on how to communicate effectively with anyone. I could explain theories of active listening, non-verbal cues, and even how to manage conflict in a relationship. But what I didn't fully understand was the emotional depth that often accompanied women's words. In early conversations with female clients or colleagues, I made the mistake of focusing too much on the words themselves and not enough on the emotions behind them.

For instance, I'd often hear phrases like "I'm fine" or "We need to talk" without recognizing the deeper emotional layers hidden within. These words weren't just statements—they were **signals** that something wasn't right. I'd respond as I would to any direct comment: offering logical solutions or dismissing the tone as an exaggeration. But as I became more aware of women's communication, I realized that **understanding her emotions** was just as important, if not more so, than understanding the words she spoke.

One of the biggest lessons I've learned over the years is that when a woman says, "I'm fine," she often isn't. She may be frustrated, hurt, or upset, but the words themselves don't reflect her true emotional state. Women, I've found, often use **indirect communication** because they don't want to appear confrontational, but the emotional need is there, waiting to be acknowledged. It was during this realization that I began to shift my approach. I stopped focusing solely on what she said, and started paying closer attention to **how she said it**, the **context**, and the **non-verbal cues** that followed.

Developing a Deeper Empathy Through Active Listening

The turning point in my understanding came when I started practicing **active listening** in a more intentional way. Active listening isn't just about hearing the words, it's about understanding the **emotions** that those words convey. It was in my personal life and in my work with couples that I started to see the **real power** of listening with empathy. When I listened not only to the words, but also to the feelings and emotional context behind them, I was able to connect in a more profound and meaningful way.

There was one specific moment in my professional life that stands out. I was working with a couple where the woman expressed feeling unheard in her relationship. She said, "He doesn't really listen when I talk. I feel invisible." For the longest time, the husband thought that he was listening, but he was only **hearing** the words and responding with logical solutions. He wasn't tuning into her emotional needs, which were what she truly needed at that moment. Once I guided him to listen for the **emotional context** behind her words, everything changed. He began validating her feelings and showing empathy, and the relationship began to improve.

This experience taught me that **empathy**—the ability to **understand** and **share in another person's emotional experience**—is at the heart of effective communication, especially when it comes to understanding women.

Understanding the Role of Non-Verbal Communication

Another turning point in my journey was realizing that communication isn't just about the words spoken—it's also about the **non-verbal** cues that accompany them. Body language, facial expressions, tone, and even silence all convey meaning. Women, in particular, often rely heavily on **subtle non-verbal communication** to express their feelings, desires, and concerns. This was something I initially overlooked in my earlier work.

For instance, a woman might cross her arms not to shut down, but because she feels vulnerable or uncomfortable. A slight frown might signal frustration or sadness, even when she's not verbally expressing it. And a pause in conversation can often be more telling than the words themselves. Learning to **read these subtle cues** was an eye-opening experience for me, and it helped me develop a deeper understanding of how women communicate.

I began to notice that when a woman was upset, she often wouldn't just say "I'm angry." Instead, she might say, "I'm just tired" or "It's not a big deal," while her body language conveyed the opposite. I realized that by paying attention to these **non-verbal signals**, I could better understand her emotional state and respond more effectively.

Conflict as a Path to Greater Understanding

One of the most challenging areas I had to navigate was **conflict resolution**. Women, I've learned, often approach disagreements differently than men. They don't just want to resolve the issue; they want to feel understood and emotionally supported in the process. Early in my career, I made the mistake of trying to fix problems without addressing the emotional needs underlying them. I'd offer solutions or try to rationalize the situation, but what I missed was the fact that, often, women just wanted to feel **heard**.

Over time, I learned that **conflict** is not something to avoid. Instead, it's an opportunity to **connect deeper**. By practicing active listening, staying calm, and validating her feelings, I could turn potential arguments into opportunities for growth and understanding. I learned that sometimes, **asking the right questions** and showing empathy—not offering solutions—was the best way to resolve conflict.

A Transformative Journey

The journey of understanding the language of women has been one of the most transformative experiences of my life. It has not only changed how I approach my professional work, but also how I communicate in my personal relationships. I now understand that communication is far more than just exchanging words—it's about connection. It's about understanding the emotions, intentions, and subtle cues that underpin our interactions.

By learning to listen deeply, recognize non-verbal cues, and empathize with emotional needs, I have been able to build more meaningful relationships. It's not always easy, and it's not always immediate, but the results are worth it. Understanding the **language of women** is about more than decoding words— it's about connecting with the **heart** of what is being said.

As you read this book and learn the language of women, remember that this journey is not just about becoming a better communicator. It's about becoming a more empathetic and understanding partner, friend, and individual. The skills you develop here will not only help you understand women better—they'll help you connect with everyone you communicate with on a deeper level.

Conclusion

Throughout this book, we've explored the intricate and powerful ways in which women communicate. From understanding the deeper emotional meanings behind their words to recognizing the subtle cues in body language, every chapter has aimed to shed light on the complex world of female communication. As you've read, you've learned not just about language, but about **empathy**, **emotional intelligence**, and the **importance of connection**.

One key takeaway is that communication with women is about much more than just the words they speak. It's about understanding the **emotional landscape** behind those words—the feelings, the unspoken messages, and the **context** in which they are shared. When you pay attention to these layers, you can build a deeper, more meaningful connection with the women in your life.

Learning to **listen actively**, **recognize non-verbal cues**, and **interpret emotional timing** are all critical skills that can transform the way you engage in conversations. By using these tools, you'll not only understand what women are really saying, but you'll also learn to connect on a more profound level, whether it's in a romantic relationship, a friendship, or a professional environment.

Remember, the journey to mastering the language of women isn't about **perfecting** your skills overnight. It's about becoming more **aware**, more **empathetic**, and more present in your conversations. This will take time, practice, and patience. But the rewards—stronger, more authentic connections and a deeper understanding of the women in your life—are worth the effort.

So, as you move forward, take what you've learned here and begin applying it every day. Pay attention to her words, listen to her emotions, and look for the subtle signs in her body language. Trust that the more you practice, the better you'll become at interpreting the language of women. Ultimately, mastering this skill will not only help you understand women better, but it will also enhance every conversation you have, leading to more meaningful and fulfilling relationships.

Thank you for joining me on this journey of discovery. I hope this book has equipped you with the tools you need to understand the language of women—

and, more importantly, to connect with the women in your life in ways that are more empathetic, respectful, and fulfilling.

References

Listed below are a number of references used to write this book as well as my personal experience.

References

1. **Gray, John.** *Men Are from Mars, Women Are from Venus: The Classic Guide to Understanding the Opposite Sex.* HarperCollins, 1992.
   This influential book lays the foundation for understanding the different communication styles of men and women, emphasizing emotional needs and the different ways in which they express themselves.

2. **Goleman, Daniel.** *Emotional Intelligence: Why It Can Matter More Than IQ.* Bantam Books, 1995.
   Goleman's work on emotional intelligence is critical for understanding how empathy, self-awareness, and emotional regulation play a central role in communication, particularly in intimate relationships.

3. **Fisher, Helen.** *The Anatomy of Love: A Natural History of Mating, Marriage, and Why We Stray.* W.W. Norton & Company, 1992.
   Fisher's book offers insight into the biological and psychological underpinnings of human behavior, especially in the context of romantic relationships, helping us understand how hormones influence communication and emotional responses.

4. **Tannen, Deborah.** *You Just Don't Understand: Women and Men in Conversation.* William Morrow, 1990.
   Tannen's classic work explores how men and women communicate differently, focusing on conversational rituals, emotional expression, and the hidden meanings behind words. It is an essential resource for understanding gendered communication styles.

5. **Meyer, John P., & Allen, Natalie J.***Commitment in the Workplace: Theory, Research, and Application.* SAGE Publications, 1997.
    This work on commitment in relationships also touches on the emotional and verbal ways people communicate their needs in professional and personal contexts, giving insight into how emotional ties influence communication.

6. **Chapman, Gary.***The Five Love Languages: The Secret to Love that Lasts.* Northfield Publishing, 1992.

    Chapman's concept of love languages provides a framework for understanding how individuals express love and emotional needs through communication, which is vital for understanding the unspoken messages in relationships.

7. **Burgoon, Judee K., Buller, David B., & Woodall, Wayne G.***Nonverbal Communication: The Unspoken Dialogue.* McGraw-Hill, 1996.
    This book delves deeply into non-verbal cues—such as body language, facial expressions, and tone—and how these subtle signals can vastly alter the meaning of verbal communication, especially in intimate settings.

8. **Friedman, Harriet.***Women and Men: A Conversation.* Oxford University Press, 1994.
    Friedman explores how gender influences communication patterns, touching on the complex ways in which women and men perceive, interpret, and respond to one another in conversation.

9. **McLean, Karen.***The Language of Emotions: What Your Feelings Are Trying to Tell You.* Sounds True, 2009.
    This resource helps to decode the emotional messages that underlie our speech, offering insights into how emotions are often conveyed indirectly in communication, particularly by women.

10. **Carnegie, Dale.***How to Win Friends and Influence People.* Simon and Schuster, 1936.
    Although not specifically focused on gender differences, this timeless classic on communication and relationship-building highlights the importance of

active listening, empathy, and understanding others' emotions—critical skills for mastering the language of women.

11. **Lau, Jenny.***The Power of Empathy in Communication.* Penguin Books, 2016. A modern guide to emotional intelligence, empathy, and listening, this book is useful for understanding how emotional connections can transform communication, especially in romantic and personal relationships.

12. **Levine, Stephen.***A Year to Live: How to Live This Year as If It Were Your Last.* Bell Tower, 1997.
This work connects emotional expression and the importance of understanding ourselves and others, promoting meaningful communication in relationships, especially in times of emotional stress or conflict.